100 RAD VIRTUES

Practical Virtues for Rad Living

by Stacy lorene cahalan

Gritty Little Book Dedication

This gritty little book is dedicated to my grandmas, Edna and Lorene, who grew up in an era when practicing virtuous living wasn't exactly a choice. They didn't have time to lay in bed at night and find new and interesting hashtags to follow. They didn't have time to assemble Pinterest boards of the life they wanted to be living or reflect on first and second career options. They didn't make vision boards.

They woke up in the morning, they put their feet on the ground and they learned how to do new things. They were gritty.

Meet Edna Margarite Youngworth (1923-2000), a mother of 5 who was a farm wife. While I don't know this to be true, I feel she dreamt of not being a farm wife. She was a voracious reader and dreamer. But guess what — she did what she needed to do because she was born in an era where that is what you did. I can close my eyes and still smell her face — the fresh smell of Noxzema. She delighted in glorious naps on the davenport and always had a good book or two in waiting. She cooked, cleaned and sewed. She often wore a funny little housecoat apron. My guess is that when she entered the gates of heaven, she traded that housecoat in for a ball gown. If city life is a heavenly option, I am guessing she is in a high-rise apartment somewhere.

Meet Lorene Rosalia Becker (1928-2017), the third of 14 kids who made it through 8th grade before she was encouraged to end her formal education to help out at home. She was the 'go-to' kid when you needed something done fast. She died proud of that fact. She was the mother of 8 and known for effortlessly doing things swiftly — sewing, gardening, whipping up dinner or rocking a cranky child to sleep. She made most things look like magic. While I am guessing she, as a cradle-to-grave Catholic, was never formally introduced to Buddhism, Lorene had a Buddhist heart. She seemed to appreciate every moment she was in...at that moment. I don't think she went to bed at night dreaming of another life. I think she went to bed at night perfectly wrung out and satisfied with a day of work being done.

Both women were born in the same generation when a lot of decisions were made for them. Both women woke up in the morning and swung their feet out of bed, stood up and made the choice to do the work right in front of them.

When things got hard, they learned and practiced new virtues. And when things got even harder, they learned and practiced new virtues.

This gritty little book is for both of these women who are a large part of who I have become as a woman. They have my heart, and I certainly hope I have theirs.

XOXO,

Stacy

Words matter

Since words matter, I wanted to start with some quick definitions.

Rad = slang word for an excellent person or thing.
Virtues = Goodness
Why 100? Well, it was a nice even number.

So yeah...100 Rad Virtues. Got it?

A Reason to Pause

While there are a lot of ways you could use this book, my primary intention when writing it was to give people a reason to pause. I wanted to create a sturdy, portable book that simplified 100 virtues into bite-sized little pieces. I wanted to create a book that would have staying power in people's lives... you know, kind of like timeless virtues.

My hope is that this book could be read over and over again as our lives twist and turn. In the end, I hope that a virtue speaks to you. I hope you see a virtue that you feel called to practice or, better yet, one that calls you to practice.

Read these words aloud.

Write them down.

Draw them.

Paint them.

Send them to a friend.

Chant them.

Reflect on them.

Pray about them.

Journal about them.

Ask yourself questions about them.

What could you do in your life to improve how you practice this virtue?

Who in your life emanates this virtue?

Have you ever acknowledged this person? If not, why not? Today could be the day!

What small changes could you make in your life to improve in this space? What could you do today...or even right now?

If you made improvements, how would you show up and land on people differently?

Is this virtue one of your strengths or weaknesses?

If one of your strengths, how could you ensure your light shines even brighter?

Do the things you say
you are going to do. Period.

Practice
ADAPTIVENESS

Respond thoughtfully
and responsibly to people
who aren't like you and
to situations that go awry.

PRACTICE
assertiveness

Stand up for the truth,
no matter how hard it is
to get your words out.

Be you. Every day.

When you think about being authentic,
who in your life comes to mind?

Practice AWe

Choose to be inspired by the small details in your life.

Practice being Beautiful ♥

Be a graceful and lovely person
to everyone you meet.

Commit to doing new and
hard things. Every day.
Even when it is hard
and may even hurt.

practice...

caring

Be that person that shows others
how to be kind, how to forgive
and how to show mercy to people
when they need it the most.

practice

Commitment

Wholehearted dedication to people,
to causes, to situations and to challenges.

practice
compassion

* Who has taught you how to be more compassionate?

When people are out of luck,
show up and be there for them.
Like pronto. ASAP. Be that person.

practice
contentment

Find comfort in what you have. Period.
Yes, this means finding comfort
in the people in your life,
the stuff you have accumulated,
your thoughts, your ambitions.
Or decide to make a change.

practice cooperation

Wholehearted willingness to help
each other be successful.

practice
being
COURAGEOUS

Never ever give up on yourself
or the road in front of you.
When you see a switchback,
brace yourself and keep going.

To make or produce something new.
To shine a new light on anything.

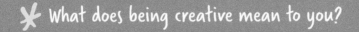 What does being creative mean to you?

practice curiosity

Challenge yourself to learn about new topics and people as if they have the power to change you for the better. Because they do.

Practice Decisiveness

When humans need direction,
be that person who shows up,
helps to weigh all of the relevant
information and feelings,
and chooses a path forward.

Challenge the status quo when
the status quo needs to be
challenged — or rather knock over
the hurdles that are stifling progress.

Practice DEtachment

A vast appreciation of the here
and now — an approach to life
and relationships that is objective, open
and resistant to unnecessary drama.

Practice

determination

Strong bent towards getting things done and working toward goals, even when things are hard.

Serve one another with a big
and whole heart, and with all
of your might and muscle.

* Today is a new day, what one thing
could you do to be a little more devoted?

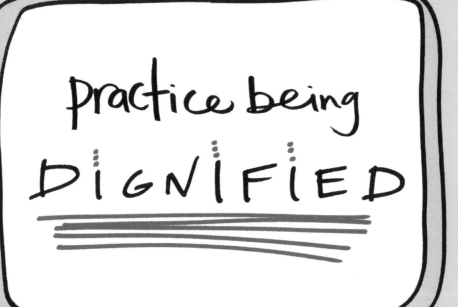

Wherever you are, act as if your grandparents are watching and analyzing your every move.

Show up with your best energy.
Everywhere you go.
With everyone you meet.

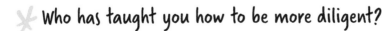 Who has taught you how to be more diligent?

Practice being

DISCERNING

Recognize things that
no one else recognizes.
Recognize differences that
make a difference —
and act on those instincts.

practice being

Disciplined ➤

Decide who you want to be.
And be that person.
Carefully curate and control
your actions and behaviors.

This is hard work.

Look around you.
Listen closely.
Put yourself in the shoes of others,
especially those that
need care and attention.

Practice encouragement...

Inspire others to be the
best version of themselves.

practice

endurance

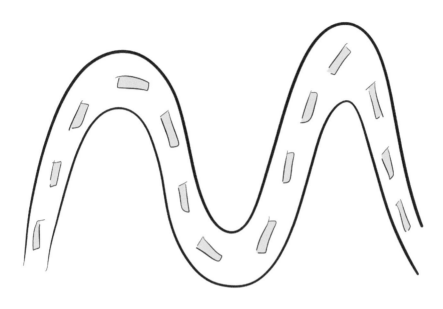

Be the last one to give up.

Practice being enthusiastic

You have one chance at living.
Show up! Be excited about it!

✳ Envision yourself waking up with a new commitment
to being enthusiastic. What changed in your heart?

Practice being

ethical

Acknowledge the difference
between good and bad.
Choose good. Make good decisions.

Surround yourself with good people and
goodness will follow you around.

practice
excellence

Set the bar high for yourself.
Set goals. Create daily practices
for crushing those goals.
Focus on you.

And then help others do the same.

Practice

faithfulness

Believe in something
bigger than you.

practice fidelity

Be honest.
All the days of your life.

When life doesn't go your way,
smile and breathe. What's done is done,
but you decide where to go next.

practice

FOCUS

Don't lose track of days or goals.

practice
forGiveness

Give people space for imperfection.

* Pause. Think about being more forgiving.
  You rested for a moment. You are amazing.

PRACTICE

FORTITUDE

An abundance of mental strength
and a commitment to brave living.

PRACTICE

friendliness

Acknowledge people around you.
Be warm. And get your head
out of your phone, dammit.

✳ Smile at everyone you see today.

practice generosity

Take care of yourself first and then look
for abundance in your life.
Give people around you the rest
of what you have to give.

✳ What gifts can you share with those around you?

Be the smile.
Be the hug. Be the light.
Be the kind touch.

Treat people as if you have no idea
what could be troubling them.

practice being
good-tempered

Be pleasant, dammit.

practice
graciousness

A generous and kind spirit that
makes people feel at ease and always
welcome in your life and home.

✳ How could you practice being more gracious?

Be present enough in this very moment to recognize everything you have right before your eyes.

PRACTICE

GRIT

An everyday tenacity that allows one to thrive in situations that suck the spirit and energy out of most people. A warrior spirit.

PRACTICE

harmony

Create balance and be happy
in your own skin. And you will
radiate harmony everywhere you go.

Own and speak the truth.
Be truthful to others and ourselves.

practice being
honorable

Recognize the privileges you
have in this world and be grateful
for them and to them.

Practice Hopefulness

Show up.
Stay positive.
You can do this.

 What does being hopeful mean to you?

PRACTICE

Humility

The perfect amount of pride
that allows your light to shine
while blending nicely
into your surroundings.

practice
being
imaginative

Create something.
Invent new ways of doing
ordinary things.

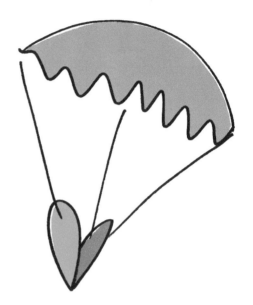

practice being
independent

Be willing and able
to take care of yourself.

Find useful skills to keep yourself
occupied. And then get busy
doing useful things for others.

Practice intiative

It's really simple — take the first step toward doing something awesome, or being someone awesome.

✳ How could you practice taking initiative?

Stay out of trouble.
Surround yourself with people
who stay out of trouble.

Practice
integrity

Make good decisions.
Surround yourself with good people.
And you will find yourself
happy and admired.

Find and celebrate happiness.

Practice being

Just

Be reasonable.
Use your head.
Treat people properly.

practice being

KiND

Be nice, dammit.

Practice being

Loyal

Find a cause, find a person,
find a job. And never give up on
that cause, that person or that job.
Show up everyday and
do your life's work.

✳ When you think about being loyal,
who in your life comes to mind?

practice magnificence

Living in an impressive way —
either in our mind, in our private
lives or in front of the world.
A bent toward lavish or grand
antics and adventures.

practice being

MAJESTIC

The ultimate combination of
beauty, magic and magnificence.
YES! Let's be that.

practice being

meraful

When people need relief from
this world, be their relief.

 Close your eyes. Breathe. Think about being merciful.
That's it. You did it.

practice
mindfulness

Be aware of your surroundings.
Be aware of people.
Use your superhero powers wisely.

practice
MODERATION

While goodness should be plentiful, some of us need to dedicate time to rationing things that need to be rationed. You know the suspects in your life (like food, alcohol, lovers or technology).

practice being

MODest

Commit to being a little better person today than you were yesterday.

practice

nobility

Be a person with solid
principles and ideals that
makes humanity better off.

practice

obedience

Where practical rules have been established, follow them.

When practical rules need to be established, be the leader and get the right rules put in place.

practice being

Be excited and receptive to ideas
other than your own.

 How could you practice being more open-minded?

practice being optimistic

Believe that there is good
in this world just waiting
for you to happen upon it.

Everything and everyone
has a purpose in our lives.
Make room for it all.

practice

PASSion...

Be intensely excited about
the causes and the people
that matter most to you.

Accept things, moments
and people as they are.
Choose not to be a self-centered
turdhead when things don't go
as planned or you run into troubles.

practice
peacefulness

Find comfort in simple,
no-drama living.

practice being

perceptive

Take the time — every single day —
to understand people and feelings.

Practice

perserverence

Create goals.
Accept challenges.
Kick ass.

Practice

PRAYER

Find your sacred places.

Spend time each day being
grateful for what you have.

Ask for help from your sources
of inspiration and guidance.

✳ Close your eyes. Breathe deeply.
A simple sigh can be a silent prayer.

practice being

PREPARED

...

Be organized and be prompt.
People like organized and prompt people.

Your ability to be practical
and disciplined — two of the
hardest things you will ever practice.

practice being

RELIABLE

Give people a reason to count
on you and prove them right.
It will be rewarding for both of you.

Practice

resilience

An ability to recover, move on,
forget, forgive. An inherent
ability to be waterproofed
when being waterproofed makes
you feel stronger.

Be considerate to everyone
around you. Treat people as you
want to be treated. Period.

✳ Envision yourself waking up tomorrow with a new commitment
to being respectful. What changed in your heart?

practice being
responsible

Make sure you do what you
say you are going to do —
and if you are really committed,
go the extra inch or the extra mile.
You will be rewarded.

practice being reverent...

Maintain deep respect
for people and for life,
never giving up a sense of awe.

practice being
righteous

Stand up for what is right
even when you feel the currents of
a wave pool are at your face.
Recognize the feeling of this resistance,
temptation and adversity.

Do the right thing for those who deserve
to have someone stand up for them.

Practice Sensitivity

The capacity (and willingness)
to acknowledge and respond
to the needs and feelings of others.

practice
Serenity ♥

Keep life simple and chase calmness —
but always be ready to shine like
the brightest star in the sky.

Avoid decisions that
add complexity to your life
and to your relationships.

✳ Today is a new day.
What one thing could you do to live a little more simply?

practice being
Sincere

Decide who you are.
Be that person.
Every day. The end.

practice being SOBER

When in doubt, act calmly.

practice being

Spontaneous

Listen to your gut.
Follow your heart.
Do something NOW that wasn't
planned, but that gives you joy.

practice being

Strong

Outlast, outlove, outwork, outrest.
And then do that again.

practice

tactfulness

Swallow your words when they aren't true, necessary or kind.

* How could you show up and land on people with a little more tactfulness?

practice

tenacity

Keep the lid on your crazy.
Be persistent in chasing your dreams
and be that friend who doesn't
give up on helping others chase theirs.

practice being

tolerant

Accept that your way of living
and being isn't the only way.

practice being

TOUGH

Find hard things.
Do them often.
Do this over and over again.

practice
tranqvility

Avoid people who make
your life complicated.

Keep your personal space full
of things that make you smile.

Find time every day
to breathe deeply.

practice

true
love

Meet people where they are
and help people discover
their superpower.

✳ How could you practice being more loving?

practice being

truthful

Show up as you. Be honest
in all of your relationships.

practice being UNDERSTANDING

Pay attention to others.
Talk less. Listen more.

Bring people together.
Create reasons for people to gather
and have meaningful conversations
about things that matter.

 When you think about unity, who in your life comes to mind?

practice being

UPRIGHT

Do good things during your
limited time on earth.
Treat your earthly vessel (your body)
with tender loving care.

Practice being

Visionary

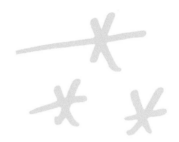

Have a plan to make your corner of
the world damn good and productive.
Don't worry about other people's corners
before you have worried about yours.

practice being wise

Be smart enough to use what
you have learned in this life and
teach others through your actions.

✳ What does being wise mean to you?

practice being

witty

Don't take yourself or others too seriously.
Find humor in the crevices
of your days. Laugh at yourself.
Laugh with — not at — others.

practice
WONDER

Never lose your ability to
find magic in this world.

✳ Do you need more wonder in your life?

practice
zealousness

Devote the hours in your day to living eagerly and with passion. This kind of life will make you a happy and grateful old person.

Published by Stacy Cahalan
Overland Park, KS 66212
www.blueraddish.com

Library of Congress Control Number: 2020918695
ISBN: 9780578729749

First Edition

Design by Lori Bennett

People in your corner.

This book happened for two reasons.

1. My Uncle Neill nudged me a year ago. He told me he thought I should put some of my art and words into a book. Uncle Neill, my hope is that this is the first of many, thanks to your nudge.

2. The first person you call when you feel accountable to Uncle Neill is Lori Suzanne Bennett. She is the creative equivalent to buying one of those turbo chargers for your phone. You meet her for coffee. You spill out your thoughts and dreams. She takes notes. You send her loads of content. You meet again. She takes notes. She sends you a game plan. And then love and magic happens.

Uncle Neill and Lori Suzanne, I am thankful for you being in my corner.

9 780578 729749